ST. BONIFACE ELEGIES

ST. BONIFACE ELEGIES

Catherine Hunter

Garry Thomas Morse, Editor

Signature
EDITIONS

Cover art by Cliff Eyland. *Low Level* NATO *Flight over Labrador.*
Acrylic on Masonite, 1990, 5" × 3".
Cover and interior design by Melody Morrissette.
Photo of Catherine Hunter by Leif Norman.

This book was printed on Ancient Forest Friendly paper.
Printed and bound in Canada by Marquis Book Printing.

We acknowledge the support of The Canada Council for the Arts
and the Manitoba Arts Council for our publishing program.

Library and Archives Canada Cataloguing in Publication
Title: St. Boniface elegies / Catherine Hunter.
Other titles: Saint Boniface elegies
Names: Hunter, Catherine, author.
Description: Poems.
Identifiers: Canadiana 20190057432 | ISBN 9781773240459 (softcover)
Classification: LCC PS8565.U5783 S73 2019 | DDC C811/.54—dc23

Signature Editions
P.O. Box 206, RPO Corydon, Winnipeg, Manitoba, R3M 3S7
www.signature-editions.com

1. SUBMISSION

2. WINTER ARCHIVE

3. THE NEWS

4. THE READER

1
SUBMISSION

Submission

Enclosed please find the night sky over West Hawk Lake,
a new moon, constellations tight and clean behind the August Perseids,
shards of broken atmosphere that blaze and vanish
miles above the jagged pines. I submit, for your consideration,
the cold, deep water, the rocky beach, the black lake sharpening
its waves against the shore.

High in my glass tower, I transmit these signals to you, tap,
tap, tap, above the vast and sparking maze of streets, long banks
of red eyes winking green. On the desk before me, a scatter
of coins and paper. A pencil stub. Two postage stamps
adrift in a clay bowl. The daily anchors. An envelope
addressed to myself.

I submit the half-read novel I abandoned on the swing, the candle
I left burning when I slipped away. I surrender also two girls
lying on the dock with sand and slivers in their hair, sunburned
faces upturned in the dark, their birthday bracelets flashing
on their wrists as they point north: meteors raining
through Andromeda's empty skull.

My work has previously appeared as a sleek white spear of light,
racing through the neon web from satellite to satellite,
remitting what I've seen and can no longer see. Like the man
who's walking on the beach, while I'm here in the city, working
late. Receive him gently, as you're not the person he's expecting.
Please find him wading through the shallows, barefoot and alone,

watching the stars fall.

After Rain

Years ago, I took my little daughter
out for walks, believing she belonged
to me, and showed her all the things
I knew the names for: dragonflies, blue jays,
chickadees, and red-winged blackbirds
swooping low across the reeds.

When she was four, she turned in her stroller
and looked up at me to ask, how
did we get here? It was summer,
the Earth turned slowly then.
I had plenty of time to answer.

Tonight, no moon, no sound.
All down the street the windows hum
with light and heat, and I'm alone
in the garden after rain. The time has come

to tell her how we got here,
but she's grown up, left home.

Who am I and what do I own?
A house and bones, a glimpse
of the blackbird's wing, the wind's dark rush,
and after the last breath, wilderness.

Chatham Beach

Remember the gifts the beach gave up? Those small
surrenders—crab shells, children's runners, seaweed
like reel-to-reel audio tape unspiralling
through a hole in a bleached-dry boat,

the striped shadow of snow fence rippling
over the ribs of sand, and the fox. Remember
the fox? Its thin black socks and spine of fire,
loping down the sloped dune of the cove.

A yellow boat and two blue boats and oars. Floats hung
from knotted ropes and a white swing hung in the lee
of a cottage porch. And a mile from the beach,
three old lighthouses dark in the dark trees. Retired.

We descended the wooden staircase to the shore. A surfer
leaned on his board and told us that last year he could still fight
the incoming tide, but he's too old now. We stood beside him,
watching younger men paddle out to ride the twilight waves.

Back home, in the northern cities where we were born, leaves fell.
The fox I once saw in the shallow valley of the Seine
fled like a burning comet under the bridge. But my mother's fox
came up the bank of the Red to be with her, to be still beside her.

Above the beach, the long, deserted tennis courts stretched
to the sky, and stars appeared in the shapes of fish and parables.
Trailers passed on the highway, their striped flags flying.
Behind us, high on the hill, the lighthouse beacon turned and turned,

and at the far edge of the beach, the fox, like a small campfire.
The wind moved in the trees like the voice of my mother,
she who loved foxes, she who has been, at last, released
into the wild, coming to tell us good night.

Holiday

FOR ANNIE

In Provincetown, we ate clam chowder at a paper-covered table
by an open window, and the other women smiled at us, believing
we were lovers. Beyond the long sill of the window, the beach,
and beyond the beach, the long pier of birds. We were on holiday,
you in your Salem, Massachusetts T-shirt, me in black. In town
we looked at postcards, cameras, kites, a fortune teller's shop.
The women strolled the streets in pairs, holding hands
and eating ice-cream, fried potatoes, lobster rolls.
You asked if I wanted my fortune told, and I said *no*. I didn't know
what a holiday was. I took a picture of the fishing boats in harbour,
and a picture of a seagull cracking clams. I took two yellow dogs
with braided leashes lying in the sun and the rusted bones
of a beach chair beside a can of beer, abandoned, upright in the sand.
Later, on the marsh, a white sail gliding in the distance over grass,
a heron lifting silver wings against the lustrous rain. Sometimes
the healing is so swift you cannot catch your breath,

and sometimes it's so slow it's imperceptible. We travelled
north to meet your cousin Tony and for hours watched him
fish for bass off the Bass Rocks of Gloucester, white gulls
wheeling through the white Atlantic spray above his head,
and every time he caught a fish, he kissed it on the lips and set it free.
Then he drove us into Boston in his silver car, and we drank martinis
at the Plaza bar, pretending we were Sylvia and Anne
and he was Robert Lowell. It was October. Years away
from this garden I'm standing in right now. You asked me
if I'd forgotten the world, and I said *yes*. The bartender told us stories
about famous people he had served, and Tony gave him fishing tips.
We ate our olives whole. We pilfered the thick white paper towels
embossed with long-necked swans. I hadn't forgotten the world,
not yet, though I knew I'd never enter it again. At the edge
of the continent, the neap tide turned, a kind of waking

or escape. This evening, a pattern of apples like a pale
solar system in the dark leaves, and every minute a deep
thump as one of them comes to ground. I'm remembering Cape Cod,
the kissed fish and the dry martini, how you led me out of my life,
and onto the earth. I'm remembering that heron, a creature much like us,
reaching up to draw new light from the sky.

Arrival

The airplane descended over Dublin,
and the dark, tidal river rose to meet me.

Mum, I said, *I made it*, but by then
my mother had already given her body

to science and would not answer.
The Ormand was closed for renovations,

and on the pedestal of the James Joyce statue,
a teenage boy wept and howled; tears and snot

streamed into his open palms. I walked past as if
he were a ghost I was pretending not to see.

I walked for miles. What is it that makes us return
to places we've never been? In Parnell Square,

an early morning worker swept away the empty bottles
offered up to the rising Children of Lir by late-night pilgrims.

In the darkness of despair, we saw a vision, said the plaque.
We lit the light of hope. At the Post Office I saw it was true

you could see the bullet holes. *History*,
said Stephen, *is a nightmare from which I am trying*

to awake. On the steps of the Bank of Ireland, Pat Ingoldsby
displayed his poetry books with a hand-lettered sign: *buy one*

and get this building free. He asked me if there was a difference
between Canadians and Americans. I thought of my parents,

two countries married to each other. Each hour, I grew heavier,
as if soaking up stories from the humid air.

I toured the National Gallery,
dreaming on my feet in vivid flickers,

finally staggered down the street
to Trinity, where I collapsed

on the grass and clover under a big-leaf maple
on the college grounds. As I slept at last,

I felt the ancient maple roots beneath me
stir and stretch themselves in all directions, seeking out

the subterranean waterways that snake and cross each other
under Dublin's streets, though I didn't know about them yet,

the way they rise and sink at intervals, burble on the surface
for a spell, then dive beneath the city pipes and graveyards

to flow through hidden, prehistoric river beds, turbulent
and deep as grief, travelling to the Liffey and to sea.

Irish Studies

FOR LOUIS DE PAOR

James Joyce's flat black wallet strapped into a glass case,
abandoned, as if he couldn't take it with him.
And what do Brendan Behan's eyeglasses
see at night, when they're all alone in the museum?

Yesterday on the train from Dublin to Galway,
I saw from the window round bundles of hay in the fields
and a golf course, two white goats
grazing on the green beside the flag.

The first time I crossed the Corrib, a man was fly fishing there,
up to his thighs in the cold, rushing water,
while all along the Salmon Weir bridge,
people leaned over the rail to watch him.

At the university, the professor advises:
engage in as complicated a way as possible
with your studies. Outside on the tall stone walls
of the building, the hoarse voices of rustling leaves.

I asked the scholars, how complicated
does it have to be? They answered in Irish,
consonants dissolving on their tongues,
leaving holes in the middles of words.

This morning in the River Corrib, two wild white swans asleep
with their necks curved back across their folded wings,
floating and rising and sinking on the waves. Two
clouds in the sky.

Connacht

At the airport, the garda had stamped my passport
with the wrong date, so technically I was illegal.

Disconnected, restless, I headed west to hear
the language my family had forgotten,

and when I found it, I found it impossible
to learn. Spent a day in Ballinasloe (a poet

I met in a cheese shop taught me how
to pronounce it), birthplace of my father's mother

and her mother, Mary Conaire, a town known mostly
for its horse fair and insane asylum. At the parish shop,

I bought a rosary for my cousin, who's always said
we're related to the celebrated, long-dead

Irish-language writer of the region, though I'd never
believed it. I travelled farther west, to the stone-hard coast,

sailed by ferry to the Aran Islands and rented a bicycle
on Inis Mór, to ride north to the ruins of Dún Aonghasa,

a fort that once loomed at the top of the cliff, a hundred metres high
above the crashing waves. Listened as a tour guide

described a nearby excavation, where archaeologists unearthed
a double grave. *Two Viking warriors*, he said—then a long, Irish

pause—*minus the heads*. I inched away from the edge
of the cliff, imagined the murderer hoisting the heads

by their hair, holding them aloft for all to gaze upon, then
hurling them out to sea—the curved trajectory of their flight,

a calculated theatre of terror. I returned to the mainland,
sunburned and certain as ever these people had nothing

to do with me. At the Crane bar, a group of poets read
from *Under Milk Wood*, and all the drinkers listened.

The poets told me they were doing it in bits,
and by Christmas they'd have read it all.

In Galway, I looked at the famous writer's statue,
had to admit he was rather like us, familiar

and yet strange, a chip in his stone nose. Later, in Cobh,
I asked the genealogists to explain which Conairs or O'Conaires

I was related to, and they said, *all of them*. I was descended
from Conchobhar, King of Connacht, they said, did I want

to purchase a likeness of the royal coat of arms? But I would not
be claimed so. Besides, I needed the extra euro for the train

back to Dublin, on which I met a poet named Patrick Quirk,
the very name of Mary's husband. He laughed and told me to look

in the phone book (one for the entire country). *You'll discover
you're related to everyone,* he said. But I didn't need to look.

I could feel it in the rumble of the train tracks, in the sunlight
that sparked off the white, rushing streams we passed,

and the salmon in the streams, the poets and the murderers,
the rabbits on the common, the swans and goats and lavender

and hundred-and-sixty-year-old big-leaf maples
on the college grounds, and the sky

through which I'd soon be travelling home
from home.

banff

beyond the glass on the third floor,
second floor, fifth—the buildings
on the mountainside are difficult
to measure, doors open
onto staggered altitudes—
valley wide as the eye can yawn.

four weeks booked at a writing
retreat, with strict orders
from the doctors
not to write.

the right arm, writing arm,
muffled in bandages, is mute,
the right hand too weak
to grasp a pen.
the left can type, but
cant manage the shift key.

i squeeze the stuffed toy frog, perform
the stretches pictured on the diagram.
apply the ice three times a day.

there is a woman inside me, painting
the underside of my skin, bright dabs
and swirls. she decorates the inside
of my skull. she dances,
in a mask and gag.

in the middle of the night
she sometimes stutters half words—
short, left-handed smudges
on a memo pad beside the bed.
otherwise, she is silent,
has no history, tiptoes

through the library, does not unzip
her backpack, only imagines
the pencil inside.

watches an eagle wheeling high
through miles of falling snow.

one night she slips away, descends
the forest staircase.

where has she gone? her voice
a negative number,

her thin inner lining discarded
at the bottom of the hill.

in the town below the town,
streets sleep under sheets of ice.

a magpie appears on a grave
stone so soft with years of rain

the letters are no longer.

the bow

when we said good-bye for a month, you
wished me good luck. *whats that*, i asked.
my right arm wasn't healing, so i didn't know
how to talk to the world. i entered
the forest on foot, followed the long
bow river to the falls, saw speckled
rainbow trout glimmer and slide
like water over the rocky slopes.
wanted to stop for tea at the banff springs
hotel, but my legs could go no higher.
cold air, pale scent of snow, and a clacking
from the golf course below, as if a giant
were knitting with wooden needles.
looked down to see two elk on the verge
of the 15th green (par 4), antlers
locked, stubborn heads knocking
against each other, unable to pull free.

therefore, this morning, i gave in. *lets escape,*
i texted fervently, left-handed. *come rescue me*
and take me to vancouver. i packed my bag,
took a bus through the park to meet your train.
all night snow fell as i slept in a jasper hotel,
rock music thumping through my mattress
from the bar below. in the morning, i waded
knee-deep in snowdrifts to the station.

by the time we reached vancouver,
it was hallowe'en. outside our window
at the sylvia, bright rockets bloomed
like peonies against the sky, a shower
of noisy long-tailed comets, and the lights
of a far-off jet plane heading west
across the ocean to the east. *why*
are we travelling, you asked.
you were half asleep. i closed my eyes,
let the fireworks repeat their patterns
on my eyelids. thought of the boy i'd seen

near lake louise, peddling a unicycle
on the icy highway, and the long-legged
wolf, so loose and lazy, striding at great speed
down the embankment to the wild
corridor of the valley. *we are all*
travelling, i guess, i said. thought
of the words that had slipped
beyond my grasp all month,
bright trout sliding over rocks.
under the skin and fat of my forearm
the ruined muscle twitched,
trying to catch them.

downtown campus

staircase
i am returning, ten or eleven steps
at every turn, to work. backpack
heavy with books, ice pack
strapped to my right arm to prevent
writing. kind students open doors
for me. without the shift key,
i become minimalist. my words
look like my teenage poems, quiet.
as the sociologists taught me, pain
shuts people up.

escalators
closed for maintenance.
stairs stilled in their endless,
opposite quests.

department office
copy machine, mailboxes, hundreds
of yellow pencils, crushed hole
in the second-storey window
made by a boy who shot an air rifle
from the apartment block across the street,
microwave oven, bulletin board. a memory
hovers between the panes, where the pellet
is still trapped. the sound when it hit glass
instead of my eye, the advantage
of storm windows.

atrium
danger, falling ice.

classrooms
safe, so far. white screens and projectors
that don't work, clocks with minds
of their own. chalk dust blizzards
after every lecture.

library
white buckets between tarp-covered
shelves collect drips from leaking roof.
orange spiral staircases lead to secret
study lofts. once, when still a student,
came down from my carrel to find
the stacks deserted. slowly felt the silence
deepen and expand. all alone. ran down
to the circulation desk. no one. raced
through the empty school as in a dream.
down, down, down the escalators.
everyone had been evacuated while
i was reading, because of a bomb
scare. there was no bomb, though. only
cancelled exams, a flicker of twilight-zone
fantasy, library all to myself, on the highest
storey in the building. full of books
and therefore closest to heaven.

Dutch Exhibit at the WAG

We have surrendered everything at the door
and can't remember what we carried here. Silence
slants across the portrait of the artist's sisters,
lays bare the scrubbed, scarred surface of their kitchen table.
I have broken out of the house and stolen
an afternoon with my daughter. This is the language
she understands: shape and texture and light.
She has entered Van Gogh's night, each star the mute
puncture of a needle pulled through canvas. Darkness
soaks into her skin, lodges deep between the bones.
The three sisters gaze. All they can do is gaze from their frame.
Unhappiness. They are still. They move. My daughter watches
their dark eyes follow her across the room. What
do they see? The light of Holland, 1837, spills
over, splashes on these limestone walls. Oh, the love
I've lavished on my little girl. She stands before
Wijnand Nuyen's *Shipwreck on a Rocky Coast*,
her green eyes drinking waves and backlit thunderclouds.
She has taken off her sandals and forgotten that they dangle
from her fingers. I start to read the exhibition catalogue,
but I only have one hour, and perhaps the four orange
oranges of Piet Mondrian don't need to be translated
into words. A chill arises from the stone floor, relief
from the sun that's beaten down on us all day. Forgive me.
When these things became available, I took them. I didn't know
how to refuse them, or how to keep them to myself.

$324.11

It's more than you expected, less
than you hoped for. It could be your ticket
home, the price of a winter coat,
plus taxes, a red wheelbarrow
of peat moss and roses, a hundred
seed packets laid out on a counter
in spring: carrots, cauliflower, dill,
nine bean rows and a hive
for the honeybee. Will it weigh you
down? Leave you light?
Make a sound like the rustle
and clink of a damaged engine
in your pocket? How much
can you afford to let go? You're rich
with regret. Though you've been robbed
and robbed again, you maintain
the appearance of equilibrium,
subtract your way through the night.
Minus minus, that's you. Value
is relative, as you've often said, yet
here it is, this reckoning, this measure
of your worth. After extravagance
and charity, it's simply what remains.
Your net. Your change. It's enough.
It's never enough. It's exactly
what you deserve.

Spring Cleaning

Suddenly, everything became too easy,
too June-day transparent, Gordon Lightfoot
gleaming on the stereo, molecules of snowmelt
levitating through the oxygen, released—
fruit let loose from the bowl, oranges
floating one two three above the cherrywood
table polished sleek as a citrus leaf, salt
shaker of crystal, bright prism of wine
goblets and sun flying in
through the open window, the crisp
pleat of curtain, the glass rubbed sheer
with paper and vinegar, a silver dish of seashells
on the sill, and inches below the ceiling a cloud
of ferns suspended over the vase of Gerbera daisies
and baby's breath, oh, and the baby
trying on noises, juggling vowels while mama
unties the kerchief from her hair, shakes
out the dust on the back stoop, says
seashells, baby, say seashells,
and baby says it, her lisp a mere
slipknot of a freckled thing,
a hummingbird's wing, slim hover
of syllables over the moment
words go tumble, drift to sky.

Anniversary

I can't imagine what you want to tell me
after all these years, but if I can find my glasses,
I'll read the note you left me on the kitchen table.
I'll read the mail and the thermometer
outside the kitchen window and this recipe
for pie. I'll see the way the light unravels
summer after summer and unknots the sky
until the mind falls open, spilling alphabets
and fuses, light bulbs, cat food, washers
for the bathroom tap and where I put that thing
I used to know the noun for and just why
and when I turned the oven on, and yet
I don't regret that we can't start again.

There's still so much I have to tell you,
but I'm in the kitchen, making lists
of words I can't use any more
and all the things we'll never
grasp the purpose for, these cherries
in their clear glass dish and the reason
for these cats. Fold the towels carefully,
misplace them on a shelf. Let the papers slide
onto the floor. Gather up the knives,
organize them by their size and then forget
what they are for. Forget, forget. You've been
released.

Two Thousand and Two

It's winter again, you said. It was April.
Snow was erasing the city, eliminating
the surface of things. We stood high
on the Main Street bridge above the broken river,
and the wind blew through me. You removed
one glove, slid your hand up the sleeve of my coat.
Under the girders of the bridge, a flock
of pigeons startled and took wing. As your bare
fingers traced the rhythm of my pulse, I saw
the pigeons rise together and then separate, fly south
to the hospital, north to the Cathedral.
Love is a division, a tearing apart. I felt the cold
burn of your skin against my skin, explaining
an equation I found difficult to learn: how two
can be split in two and become one. You took my hand.
I wanted to move deep into winter with you.

It's winter again, you said. It was March.
I was remembering the night you followed me
four city blocks through a blizzard when I was angry
and mean and never wanted to speak to another man again
as long as I live I mean it so help me god, but you kept walking
one two three four blocks, a wind-chill factor of two thousand
and two, and every time I turned around I saw you
coming after me. Love seemed simple as arithmetic,
a kind of subtraction. You followed me from Ellice
to Portage from Portage to Graham from Graham
to St. Mary, and on the corner of York and Garry,
I stopped and let you reach me. Love is elementary,
a peeling down to the square root.

It's winter again, you said. It was February.
We stood on the footbridge in Kildonan Park.
Skate blades scraped and scribbled on the creek.
Icicles hung from the diving board, and in the middle
of the day I became confused, the pale solar disk
so cool in the white sky I mistook it for the moon.
I saw the two small clouds of our breathing mingle,
disappear. I couldn't remember what summer was.
Winter had pared me to a sliver. Little crystal needles
laced holes in my brain. You opened my fist. We both
looked down at my empty palm. I couldn't remember
what I'd been holding on to.

It was winter again in January. Then, in December,
it was winter again. I looked south, naming the bridges
between our houses: Redwood, Disraeli,
Louise, Provencher, Norwood, every steel arch
of the river's rib cage a cold blade sharp enough
to clean me to the bone, and love unmade me,
took me deep into the dead of winter, straight
through its polished lens. I saw the wind uncolour the city,
the rivers buckle the land. I saw our friends lay down
their lives, one by one through that terrible season,
until I was numb, felt nothing except
your hand on my wrist, pulling me through.

On October thirty-first, the snow began to fall.
It's winter again, you said again.
I looked north, because north is the direction
you come from, and north is the direction you travel
when you move away from me. Love is a counting
or counting down: Norwood, Provencher, Louise,
Disraeli, Redwood. The rungs of a river as long
as winter. A river you crossed when I was still
and white with grief. You unfolded my fingers,
broke me open, and when you had stripped me
utterly naked, you touched me again.
I fell. I sank below zero.

Now, there is nothing more that can be taken
from me. Look at the sky, darkening
toward spring. The trees that open, forgiving.
The students who jump up and down
in the courtyard, clapping their hands for sheer
love of the light at seven o'clock in the evening.
None of these things can ever be lifted away—
not even this weightless light, this temporary joy.
Because everything that is mine I have already given over.
Because you followed me one night all the way
to the corner of Garry and York. Because
you took my hand. You moved with me
through winter.

Oodena

Every morning the bus flies past the hospital,
climbs the bridge above the intersection
of the rivers, and we all look out to see
the elm trees leaning from the banks as if to drink.
At the centre of town, there's an observatory
for invisible things: constellations at noon,

wind sculpture melodies, and husbands
with their minds on darker matter, who vanish
without warning. It was twilight. Canada Day.
Children flittered through the underbrush
with sparklers. Hundreds of people
pushed onto the bridge to watch

the fireworks, and somehow in the crowd
you lost your way. Afterwards, I searched
for you along the river banks, in the nearby bars.
Dialled our number, listened to the dark house
ring. Said to myself, *oh well, you always knew
you couldn't keep him.*

Years later, after a baseball game,
we were walking home together
through The Forks. *This is where you got lost
that time*, you said. *Remember?*
At the centre of town, there's an aperture,
a flaw in the Earth's electric field.

*

At Oodena, George plays "Maple Sugar"
on the fiddle. Across the river, the neon
cross above St. Boniface General marks
the site our daughter first appeared to us,
the place I touched my mother for the last time.
Ran my fingers through her soft white hair.

That's where I visited my old friend Patrick,
bringing books and flowers. Or tobacco,
when they let him come outside to smoke.
At the exit to the psych ward, he lifted
his hands, fingered the bright holes in the air,
deep fissures where a man might disappear.

North of the burnt Cathedral, the narrow Seine
comes twisting toward the Red.
At the centre of town, three waterways
converge, like my two brothers and me,
each entering the hospital on the same night
through a different door, wandering

our separate corridors through the labyrinth
until gathered once again into our mother.
Only her beautiful body at rest in a room
and a stranger saying a prayer.
Above the rivers, the bright, invisible socket
of departure was still open.

*

At Michael and Rebecca's wedding,
the bridesmaids were so young we held our breath.
At church, we heard the Song of Songs,
and later at the rowing club, the band played
"Do You Love Me?" while the guests
all did the mashed potato. They did the twist.

I stepped outside, onto the terrace, felt
in the warm night air the closeness of those things
I need no light to see because I know they're there:
the docked boats and the rail bridge,
the sundial in the darkness telling time,
the oak and elm trees and the paths that weave

among them, and the hospital grounds, where
Patrick unfolded his paper-winged poems,
the fervent itinerary of his future. Told me
he was cured at last. He was going to run away
to sea, learn to parasail, climb Mount
Kilimanjaro. *Love is a kite*, he said. He carried

no more than a sparrow carries through the air,
slipped easily into the slender opening between
the words. *Love is a fig tree, a solar wind.*
The wedding band played "Shake,"
and the wedding guests were shaking it.
I heard the river flicker like a flame.

*

Light from the windows cast gold bars
upon the water, revealed a figure on the pier
below. Then a sudden turbulence and rippling.
Another figure running with a flashlight.
Two men bent low together, struggling,
pulling something, pulling something in.

Catfish, said Ravi, who came out to watch.
We saw the flashlight's flash, a brief
illumination flapping on the dock,
and then the man leaned down
and must have tugged the hook out,
for we saw him fling the catfish through the air.

Silver gleam of its body in the beam of light,
white splash of life and it slid below the surface,
going home. Then Ron came out
and Carolyn came out behind him.
We heard the rumble of a freight train
travelling west and then another, travelling east.

A riverboat paddled south against the current,
ablaze with booze and rock and roll.
We stood on the terrace, Ron and Ravi,
Carolyn and me. Before us, two trains passing
on the trestles high above the rivers. Behind us,
Rebecca, dancing in her white dress.

*

When my daughter broke into the world
it was November, the power of the rivers
locked beneath the ice. Still, she found
her way. She is a navigator. I have seen her
thread a pathway through the woods,
blaze trails through mathematical equations.

At the centre of town, the naked-eye
observatory teaches us the stories of the stars.
Stone markers frame the sunrise
at the winter solstice, sight on Vega, point out
solar north—a direction you might need someday.
The art of calculating where you are demands

a known location. A familiar place, however
distant, to help you take your bearings.
When my mother left, I could not follow,
could not find the passage she had forged,
though I knew it was right here. If only
I could sight a line among the oaks and elms,

triangulate the vectors of the rivers, measure
the magnetic declination. Instead, I learned
what I didn't want to learn, passed
through a lesser opening, became
somebody else. Lost and working
in a world that I don't recognize.

*

They say the northern pass
is the best route up Mount Kilimanjaro,
the wildest one, the most remote.
Elephants graze on the grasslands
of the lower slopes, and leopards
prowl the montane forest, hunting antelope.

They say the planet's warming up. The ice fields
at the summit have begun to melt. The trees are thirsty,
fires sweep the upper timber line. Yet still
the mountain holds its ark of families, its delicate
wild flowers, heather and lobelia, rare black rhinos,
herds of wild dogs and gazelles.

Still the stars above
Uhuru Peak are breathing,
close enough to touch.
Patrick's probably on his way by now.
He's on the foot slopes with a walking stick,
beneath the rubber trees.

Tomorrow he'll emerge above the clouds
onto the moorland, where
the air's so thin desire finally
dissipates completely.
He'll climb the alpine desert
to the snow.

*

I keep in my house a gift that Patrick gave me,
a pale pink alabaster elephant with a smooth hole
through its belly. He didn't know
it was a napkin ring. It lives
in the china cabinet with the teacups
and the other elephants, the brass one

and the one my daughter made of clay
when she was little. Even then
we knew she was a person who could coax
the earth into her hands and give it shape.
I've seen her walk into a room,
my mother's necklace sparkling at her throat.

I've seen her light the kindling
in the garden fireplace and wake the flames.
The evening she was born, snow fell
against the window of the taxi as I paid the driver.
That's the last thing I remember from that other life:
snow that burst like fireworks

above the hospital, the neon sign, the glass
doors leading to Emergency. I knew
I needed to enter those doors, but first
I stood in the parking lot a moment, alone
for the last time, raised my head
to watch the cool white sparks escape the darkling sky.

2
WINTER ARCHIVE

Theft

And now, beyond the television,
beyond even the front window
of your little house, out on the snow
at the edge of the Seine, in the vacant
lot across the street, a car is burning.
This is a test, but you don't know it yet.
A 1995 Thunderbird in flames.
No, it's not some emblem of your lost youth,
a sign of recklessness, abandon. It's simply
a stolen car that pulled up while you were not
paying attention. The blank iced surface of the river
begins to glow, as if combustible. You rise
from the couch and wake your husband.

When the electrical system catches fire,
the tail light blinks and the horn sounds,
as if someone trapped inside is signalling
for help. You dial 911. Then it all becomes a blur.
That's what you tell your friends afterwards,
it was all a blur—two o'clock in the morning,
your brain full of sleep and television.
Later, you remember what you saw,
though you don't speak of it. Your naked husband
running across the street, as if he could pull that unseen
person out before the gas tank blew.
But nobody was in the car. That's the point,
as you like to repeat: there was nobody
in the fucking car. The trouble is you can't forget
your husband's body in its skin against the flames.
How willing it was, to leave you for a stranger.
And now, when he touches you, you're cold.
There's a mean stripe of heat across his palm
where he tried to open the handle,
but it does not warm you. When he drinks
too much, when he swims too far from shore,
when he rides his bicycle with no hands, his two arms
open to the wind—you can feel how cold you are.

At first, all you can think of
is that moment when you were twelve
years old, your toes gripping the rough
edge of the ten-metre diving board,
wondering if you'd go over, and when,
whether you'd survive. Then you remember
those hot diamonds in the chamber of mirrors
at the planetarium, that deep, deep, glittering
space in six directions, yourself suspended, falling.
You are going down again, and why? You're leaving
behind the slight drift of cumin and ginger
from the rooms below, the dull pulse in your thigh,
a distant radio. Outside, there might be a wind-chill
factor of fifteen hundred or a flood
or another boy smashing a stolen car
into your fence, but you have already gone
too far to know these things or care what time it is.
Down here, it's always the middle of the night.
It's crowded as a dream with ladders,
closets, open doors, steep stairs for your
inevitable descent. Your dead friends gather,
watching over your shoulder, muttering
translations of the words your pencil's forming
and reforming. There are strangers down here, too.
Sometimes they ask for help, as if
you could rescue them. Or they lead you on,
pretending to know the location of your keys,
your sock, that letter you think you wrote
but did you mail it? Why do you enter
and enter again this space where the laws
of logic bend like sunlight clinging
to the curves of matter? You keep on
travelling deeper, though by now you know
full well there are no insights here.
There are only mismatched gloves, stopped
watches, overdue books. Then darkness,
an inflorescence of stars, a splintering.
It was long ago you realized you're not

looking for anything down here any more.
You are one of the lost objects. No one
is coming to find you.

The Headache

The skull sparks, impatient in the blindness
of the bedroom, and though the shades are drawn,
the left socket cracks open under the closed eye,
drinks light through the skin of the lid.
What is it telling you, this bright throb of blood
through the temple? You guess it's the same old
story of the end of things, and you don't want
to listen. *Listen.* When you were twelve
you fell on the skating rink and saw above you
the forked, hoarfrosted branches of lightning
like a maze, and when you were nineteen
you stepped into the road too quickly
and saw that long tunnel of light, studded
with snow and shards of headlight glass,
and when you were twenty-six you split in two
and they drew out of your body the radiant
living soul you call your daughter. And now
they are showing you again the white flame,
saying, *be prepared.* You know this flame.
It belongs to you, and nothing is as lonely
as possessing it. Your daughter enters,
lays a cool cloth on your forehead, where it steams,
disintegrates into a sheet of ash. You think you hear
her voice, but you can't see through the glare,
and when she vanishes into the hot corona,
you see clearly there can be no preparation.
But you won't remember what you saw. The headache
won't last, not this time, not yet. Tomorrow you'll rise
from the bed and bathe and dress and walk
into the winter streets. You'll count your coins
and buy a loaf of bread, a paper. See?
You're sitting on a park bench, reading
while the flakes of snow are whirling.
All morning, all around you,
the pale and temporary
darkness that's your life
is closing in.

Voice

When you send it out of the body to seek
the shape of a room, it unfolds

into four dimensions of morning, measures
every plane and curve of ceiling.

The voice is not a hand, or an eye, and yet
it performs for you an accurate atlas of your

boundaries, tells the precise shape of the distance
between door and table, between two lovers.

At night, when the eyes close, and the hands
let go of the day they have held, the voice moves

beyond the confines of the bed. Maybe
in those dark moments, the voice looks back and sees

the body that housed it, the prison cell
from which it has escaped. Or maybe the voice,

in its sculptural intelligence, sees its own condition
without metaphor. It sighs out of the cramped room

where you're sleeping, whistles through the keyhole
of the house, explores the city streets. What does it praise

when it's released? What does it predict, protest?
It curls around the singing teacher's house and purrs.

It gathers power as it surges down the river, filling its sails,
then lifts off toward the clouds. Maybe a storm is on the way.

When your lover tells you you've been talking in your sleep,
he claims he can't make out the words, but can you trust him?

Is he communing with your voice at night? *Voice*, you say,
who do you think you are? And the voice says, *Shh.*

Landmarks

You walk out of Don's Photo and turn the corner.
Now you are expected to describe the weather: high
cranes over the avenue, jackhammer and drill,
another operation on the drugged body of the city.
Transplant, amputation, root canal. Multiple grids
of your hometown overlap in memory.

You pass the bookstore that was once
a music store, the empty lot that was
your father's office. You pass the school
for ballet dancers that was once an old hotel
where you drank beer with Patrick, who once
was Patrick. And behind that hoarding
on the south side of the avenue, what belonged
there? The library's been erased, redrawn.
A thin survivor crouches in the snow, baseball cap
in his bare chapped hand. And where's Eaton's?
You've been away. Or maybe
you've been sleeping. You're waking
slowly in an unfamiliar place. You follow
the run-on line of river, cross the renamed bridge,
carrying the envelope of photographs—traces
of your travels in the world beyond.
You pass the graveyard, burned-out church,
and detonated abattoir. You're coming home.

In the kitchen: orange peels, the loose fallen petals
of valentine roses he gave you, red. The newspaper
speaks of children stealing cars, breaking into schools
to swipe the hockey gear, or selling themselves
for crystal meth. Citizens are outraged.
Will someone have to die, they cry,
before something is done? And once again time
turns inside out, right here in the kitchen. A radiant sphere,
a small other planet, in which all the children are still
alive, floats like a transparent bubble high above
the radio. Astonishing resurrection. The power
of forgetting. You sweep up petals and peels, make tea.

Outside, the ebb and flood of the over-mapped wind,
the flying snow—yes, all right, the weather.
Return to your work, constant reconstruction
of story, hammer and stitch and headache,
smeared ink, tangle of lines, and over it all,
a keen desire to steal a car, speed through streets
to the Trans-Canada highway, follow those kids
into the sweet, indifferent wind. Instead,
you struggle to recall the moment—some mute
and stubborn moment—when it all went wrong,
to recite, correctly, the names of the dead,
the list that's always trembling like a pulse
beneath the page, thready and dangerous
as a dull knife.

Guests arrive for dinner. Spread the photographs
across the table, show them where you've been:
Lunenburg Memorial, Ottawa war museum, the high
bridge above the Don Valley Parkway, with its ad
for a crisis line—toll-free number suspended
over the void. And last, from a train window,
naked birch trees on the banks of the Vermillion,
the white shock of their reflection in the river,
ghosts that followed you home.

Later: slurred moonlight. Winter constellations
floating like a net above the roof. Nobody speaks
of the country that made us, the city we share,
its chronic amnesia. *O*, as Patrick would have said,
impermanence. Everyone eats cake, drinks wine, while
outside in the dark, winter tightens its metal mesh
of street lamps. *So, what are you working on?* they ask.
Failed escape routes, works on paper that disintegrate
each dawn among shifting monuments and weather,
pulverized as dust in the cracks of sandblasted buildings.
Sharpen a pencil, begin again:

Winter Archive

From the airplane window, stripped
trees and a frozen lake, a shape
you recognize from aerial photography,
and all along the eastern shore, a carapace
of ice that's melted and re-melted, slick
and flashing like a mirror. Then the clutch
of silver buildings trapped inside the floodway,
peaked roofs flattened by the sharp blue air
and locks on every door. Your city from the sky,
oblivious and in danger and as usual not thinking
of you, unaware of your descent. Remember
the boy who tunnelled deep into the drifts
and died unseen, his crushed lungs full of snow.
And the boy who cut across the river late
in March and sank below the ice, the flutter
of his woollen scarf as he surrendered.
Lower now, you sail above the zoo and see
below you in the bright, bleached field,
huddled tight against the February wind,
a small herd of camels.

Tonight, steel mesh of constellations
and a die-cut moon. Flames
in the northern sky and sirens—
another fire in an old hotel. Every
hour on the hour, you wake
and listen to the spectral speech
of freight trains arcing
through the troposphere,
arguments of snowploughs
with the wind. With a pencil you perform
a night translation, composing
in your sleep. You thought you might
transcribe the weather, document
the customs and geography,
the architecture of the place,
but in this city nothing lasts
for long, the memory not a storehouse

but an exhalation, crystallized. The breath
of a boy locked out and forced to wander
through the streets on New Year's Eve, alone.

You don't know why they're haunting you,
these phantom children and their deadly
accidents, escapees from a film
you watched in elementary school
each year before the holidays, grim
lessons about winter safety.
In this morning's paper, tales
of robbery and arson, stolen cars.
A photo of the burnt hotel,
its transformation overnight
into a palace made of icicles,
an arctic fairy tale about amnesia.

You didn't want to see the movie,
but the teachers made you
look. Dark scratches quivered
on the screen as one by one
the children met their fates
in black and white. Remember
the girl who rounded the curve
of the creek too fast, the silver blades
of her speed skates shaving ice, frost
rising from her heels like steam and then
the crack and snap of bone. The girl
who slithered down the snowbank to the road
and never saw the vehicle that splintered
her toboggan and her spine. The boy
who would not wear his hat.
What were their names?
The tenth child, spared,
turned from the camera's eye
and walked away, nobody left
to play with.

After school we all stood smoking
in the sugar shacks behind the hockey rink,
forgetting. Then the boys went bumper-shining,
sliding on the glazed soles of their hard white
moccasins behind the cars while drivers
cursed and honked, and the girls hitchhiked
downtown. In Metro Park we traded cigarettes
and gum and glue and lemon gin and pills
that made the songs of birds come true.

The safety rules of winter: seal off
the intersection at the centre of the city,
and bury Metro Park beneath an avalanche
of earth. Reroute the river and rename
the bridge. Sandblast from the buildings
any messages the children painted there
to tell us who they are. Remove
the statue of the rebel from the legislative
grounds. Then raise the girders
and construct another monument
to juvenile detention. Take the histories
of the children, file the files away.

But the children keep returning. At night
they wander through the crooked corridors
where you keep the things you haven't quite
forgotten, their bodies grey and quivering
with static, still haloed gently
in the school projector's unreliable light.
Or in their hot-wired cars they speed
through midnight side streets, never
reaching the perimeter before the crash,
the Trans-Canada Highway not an exit but a theory
of escape, mere rumour of a continent
outside the moat, beyond the Christmas
ornaments and white, fluorescent offices.
Traffic lights count off the interstices
of the grid that bolts you in. In every window

on the residential street, a dim blue eye
is watching. From the top of the Salter Street
bridge, you've seen the sign: Winnipeg Cold Storage.
You're not going anywhere but here,
the twenty-first century, this remade town.
Every winter they screen the safety film,
and nightly they lower the cage of stars,
while high above the man-made lakes,
the power lines resume their song.

Early this morning you came east
toward home, travelled the length
of Portage to the cancelled matrix
where it crosses Main, and lo,
from the window of the number fifty
bus at dawn, you saw at last
the gateway to the underworld,
the trapdoor in the cold cement
where caribou emerge into the sun
to ford the rushing river, rearing high
their mighty heads to see
the Bank of Montreal.
A city worker with a yellow
push broom sweeps snow
from their bronze flanks.

What does it mean when animals arise
from the subconscious of a city? You knelt
by the frozen shore, dipped your hand
in the river of polished stone. Its flat
black mirror offered nothing but your own
pale face, the towers of commerce
shimmering behind you. It's February,
far too soon to think about deliverance.
Under the pavement lie the buried archives
of the city, vaults of gold, shopping malls,
secret chambers where the children gather
to evade the wind. Deep below the mayor's office,

they are sniffing solvents, eating junk
food, and perhaps inventing for themselves
fake accidents explaining how they got here.
How the world caved in. They're buried deep,
the living and the dead, the real and the imaginary
children, the ones you never knew
and those you loved, the ones you'll never
see again. You can't carry them inside you any longer,
waiting for some new instructions, some way
to keep them safe this time. And you can't
describe this city anymore, its countless transitory
revelations and illusions, all its vanishings. Erase,
redraw, rewrite for fifty years, you can't recover
all the overlapping cities that you've lost. Still,
like the last child in the safety film, the lone
survivor, you keep trying to make it home.

3
THE NEWS

Romance

I miss you. Sparrows gather at the feeder, spill
seeds and gossip, plant a field of sunflowers
in the middle of the lawn. Suddenly, your bicycle,
still locked to the fencepost where you left it, crashes
to the ground, and all the birds take flight.
The bike lies sideways, one wheel spinning.
Meanwhile, you're five miles from here,
shuffling through hospital corridors, attached
by rubber tubes to an iv pole, an astronaut
too loosely tethered to the ship. When I said
you should go wireless, you laughed. You stood
at the window, six floors above the street and waved
goodbye. Radiation, says the doctor, is just sunlight.
She tells us how precisely they will aim the beam
into your brain. Long ago, my fourth-grade teacher said
the sun is ninety-three million miles away, and we can never
escape the atmosphere of Earth because of gravity.
Now they're sending cameras out on rocket ships.
Today the Curiosity beamed home an image of the dark
sand dunes of Mars, sunlit as our backyard garden.
Beauty, said Keats, is all we need to know,
but we weren't listening. Here on Earth, the black cat
circles the honeysuckle, tangling her leash eight times
around the branches, and though it's daylight, I can see
the three-quarter moon through the cottonwood branches,
a skim-milk moon, a pale suburban joke, and I can't believe
we ended up living out here, among the landscaped lawns
and stuccoed bungalows, where we said we'd never even visit,
where the mallards criticize the neighbour's hot tub,
and a squirrel on the high wire launches a complaint—
his debut appearance on Facebook ruined
when he was misidentified as a chipmunk. Do you ever
wonder how we end up where we are? On Earth, or Mars,
or even farther, light years from the ninety-three
million miles that, way back when, seemed deeper
than a brain could go.

Liberty

So windy this spring, the apple blossoms
only lasted two days, and I forgot
to take a photograph for you. Instead,
I bring a thermos of soup, the sports news,
remind the nurses to brush your teeth. Alone
in the house all night, I'm free—not only singing
the Daniel Boone theme song to the cat
while washing dishes, but providing
cultural analysis of the lyrics as well.
I can work ten, twelve hours at a time
without your interruptions, your requests
for mustard and crossword-puzzle
answers, your advice to be reasonable
about the wine. Sweet liberty. But last
night, when the great grey owl swooped
across the yard—rush of its muscular
wings brushing my hair—there was no
witness. And tonight, I'm the only one
watching this TV concert of songs
by Leonard Cohen. All I remember
about being thirteen is listening
to "Good-bye Marianne" on the scratchy
portable record player my parents gave me,
and now on TV here is Cohen's son, all
grown up, singing that same song,
clear and rich through our digital receiver
and the kind of speakers my parents
could never afford. When we were young
and philosophical, we used to say,
time is an illusion, never dreaming
it was true. Alone in the house
these nights, all grown up, I do
whatever I want, stay awake
til six a.m., clean closets, sort
the bookshelves alphabetically
and then by genre, work the entire
crossword by myself, then nap
in the sunny spot you always reserved
for the cat. Come back.

Justice

It's 33 degrees (above, this time),
and the crisis counsellors are out
on strike. Each morning I wake
with my head glued to the pillow
by heat or maybe the simple g-force
of this carbon-based life. Flat
on my back, I watch a sort of world
through the window, or what used to be
the world. The red squirrel leaps
from roof to tree. As always,
here comes that mid-air moment
of terror between eavestrough
and thin end of the bough.
The morning radio is asking random
citizens their views on justice,
and I remember when I used to correct
my students on their use of the word
random. That was in another life, when
words had meanings that were literally
fixed as stars. The squirrel, a pirate,
bravely boards the bird feeder.
Chickadees scatter. Finches squinch. Robins
walk the plank. The squirrel clings
to a branch by some invisible means,
lowers her body and, hanging upside down,
eats fulsomely, as those who don't know
what *fulsome* means might say. And who
could blame her? Last night in Emergency,
I heard the guy in the next bed talking
to his sister, confessing to a robbery
and begging her to take the stash.
I was waiting there for hours,
as his visitors went in and out
behind the curtain. I heard him tell
three different stories: one to his mother,
one to the cops, and one to the doctor
who stitched his stab wounds
shut. I'm the only one who knew
that he was lying every time. Later,

as the cops drank coffee in the corridor,
I saw the sister walk right past them
with her pockets full of stolen drugs.
She thanked them politely
for saving her brother's life
and then she got into a cab.
I felt it was only right, maybe
a kind of justice, getting to see
the end of that story, 'cause I couldn't
see the end of ours and maybe didn't
want to. Hard to tell if that squirrel
is afraid or confident, suspended there,
but that's where stories end sometimes, mid-
air

Collision

Rain falls on the plum tree
and the catnip patch. Rain
falls on the gravesite
of the hawk who crashed
into our window in July.
Rain fills rain barrel, wheel-
barrow, bird bath. But we're dry
inside, watching people on TV
watch people on TV watch
television: the presidential debates.
It's the autumn of 2016. Nobody
is really sure how close to death
we are, but Voyager has long since
crossed the border of the solar system.
Each day it's sailing farther
into interstellar space. Rain
falls on the garden gnome
the neighbours gave me for my 50th
birthday. That night my brother
and I clicked glasses, saying,
"how in hell did we ever
get this far? How did we get in
so deep?" Stayed up till dawn,
counting the many friends
we had outlived. The hawk,
looking into our window,
must have seen the ferns
suspended from our ceiling,
must have seen the reflection
of the Scotch pine branches
in the yard, and above them,
the reflection of the blue, wide-
open sky.

Education

The anatomical charts on the doctor's wall
outline the systems of the human body: digestive,
respiratory, skeletal. My eyesight isn't sharp enough
to read the names of all the bones. I recall
the ulna and the tibia from school, but I'm not sure
where exactly they're located. Our bones are hollow,
the grade-five teacher taught us, or were those only
the bones of birds? Birds had four-chambered
hearts, and the solar system had nine planets,
and I used to think that she knew everything.
From what distant reaches are these muddled facts
arriving in this waiting room? I liked that teacher.
She let me skip out of English class. *There's no reason,*
she said, *that you should have to sit through this.*
She took us to the pool for swimming lessons.
I swam laps in the deep end, practised the butterfly stroke
and learned to dive from the three-metre spring board.
The lifeguards said there was a window way below
the surface, where they stood to watch the divers,
just in case of injury or drowning. I made sure
to rise through the water as slowly as I could. I knew
about the bends from television. I knew about quicksand—
if stuck in quicksand, Tarzan warned, do not resist.
You should stay still and wait until he rescued you.
I knew about TNT and boa constrictors, and meteors
plummeting to Earth. The grade-six teacher told us meteors
can't hurt us. They burn up when they hit the atmosphere
and drift to ground as harmless ash. We looked at each other
sideways. We'd seen the movies. At the pool, kids weren't allowed
above the three-metre tier of the diving tower, but sometimes
the lifeguard took me to the very top to give me lessons.
My first time up, I crawled on my belly to the edge. I could see
all the way through ten metres of air and sixteen feet of water
to the hard blue tiles below. At home, we sat on the living room
carpet and ate a bucket of fried chicken, watching the astronauts
land on the moon. It was my mother's birthday, and she said
they were doing it especially for her. At school next day
the principal said that any one of us could be

an astronaut someday. We discussed this possibility
among ourselves. Would you risk leaving Earth
forever, just for the thrill? We didn't know
that where we were going was scarier than outer space
and colder. On TV, the boy with the magic boomerang
stopped time so he could save innocent people from crooks,
and sometimes even death, but it was a lonely job
because nobody ever knew he'd done it. I knew
what it meant to be frozen, standing a long time
with my toes extended beyond the edge
of the ten-metre platform, feeling the rough weave
of the matting under the soles of my feet.
I bent my knees, pushed off, and for a brief, upward
moment believed I might tear free.
Then the magnetic grip of Earth—no one
has ever held me tighter—and the plunge, water
rushing hard against my eardrums until finally
gravity released my body, let me rise again.
Sometimes on purpose I kicked down deep
and deeper, to touch the clean, tiled floor.
That's when I saw the window—a bright, white
square of light, its edges fuzzy with chlorine.
I waved and waved but nobody appeared
behind the glass. And so far no one's called us in
to see the doctor, though I've studied every chart
and you've filled in every puzzle square. *Time,*
said the lifeguard, *is of the essence.* Your eyelids flutter.
You need to sleep. *Time,* said the music teacher,
waits for no one. How is it I can hear my teachers' voices
when I'm travelling from them faster than the speed of sound?
Yesterday, the Parker Solar Probe began its journey
to the Sun. *Time travel is impossible,* the physics teacher
said. Yet here we are.

Collaboration

Three doors and seven locks can't keep
the summer darkness out. It trickles in
and seeps from room to room, finds me
still awake past midnight, reading articles
on politics and art and new directions
in oncology. This tablet isn't bright enough
to wipe the dark away. It sheds a pool
of light too shallow to extend to the horizon
of the bed. Yet it illuminates. It tells me
of an artist who attached white LED lights
to the ankles of two thousand pigeons
and trained them all to fly on cue above
the Brooklyn Navy Yard (where my father,
as a kid, snuck in to watch the men build ships).
Years ago, the pigeons carried military messages
in times of war, and some of them were decorated
for their bravery. *Pigeons*, says the artist,
are *constantly observing us* and *making notes*,
and I think of the six pigeons who wrote six
tender telegrams to Hatrack the Horse, a story
I listened to, over and over, when I was a kid.

All this gives me an idea—I need some birds
to help me with my work. Trouble is,
all the city pigeons I know have their own
art projects. They roost downtown, debate
aesthetics up on high-rise roofs with vistas
vast enough to serve their visions, plot
their choreography. Or huddled in their green rooms
under bridges, they decide on arabesque designs,
perfect the timing of their sudden "startled" risings.
They're sophisticated. They're professionals. Here
in the suburbs, birds seem more approachable,
but they, too, set their own agendas. A great blue heron
in the rushes meditates, with one leg in the creek, on stillness.
Red-winged blackbirds, on patrol along the ditches
by the highway, escort trespassing crows
out of their territory. Over in the Safeway parking lot,

the gulls are squabbling over french fries, pizza crusts,
the mustard-stained remains of white buns tossed
by lunchers gobbling furtive burgers in their SUVs,
while down the street, the Canada geese assemble
on the shore of the fake lake, to fertilize the lawn.

They have no interest in my invitation to collaborate.

Two a.m. Click on the artist's video:
twilight in Brooklyn. Across the East River,
pinpoints of electric light delineate Manhattan
with that artificial golden orange that only cameras
see, those moments just before night settles in.
The artist stands on the deck of an aircraft carrier,
surrounded by pigeons of blue and white and mottled
grey and sandy brown, who flap and strut and wait
until the humans raise black flags, and then the birds
all rise together, and you hear the people gasp and cheer.
Hundreds of white and coloured wings spread open
on the air. The white bulbs on their ankles, dim at first, glow
brighter as the sun sets, until finally they're the only
things you see, brighter than the stars and moving faster,
flashing in balletic traces, curves and dips, a multitude
of shifting constellations. The birds are messengers
of light. They fly as sparks fly, upwards, born to trouble,
lifting their hollow bones, their feathers light as breath.
I watch them writing on the sky, stories I listen to, over
and over, finally drifting into sleep and a long-lost
memory: pelicans swooping low across the lake. Remember?
How close they flew beside us? I was kneeling in the bow,
while you steered between the islands, and it seemed
we were flying with them. In my sleep I feel the wind
among the white wings, feel us, all of us, skimming
the water, speeding home together, until I'm woken
by the songbirds at the backyard feeder, singing
in the dark. Even though the sun is still invisible,
they know it's coming up.

The News

Today the missionaries left a flyer
in our mailbox: *the light shineth*
in the darkness and the darkness
comprehends it not. But it's too late
now for us to start believing. We toss
the flyer on the garden fire, watch it burn
in silence. Ever since the diagnosis,
we've been quiet when alone
together. Still, we have our rituals.
Out on the deck tonight, we toast
the rise of Jupiter with a glass
of white. Then both our phones light up—
it's our neighbours, relaying
the latest news about the songbirds.

All summer we've watched them at the feeder,
looked up their names in *Birds of Canada*:
tanager, warbler, dark-eyed junco, cedar
waxwing. Tonight's news is they're dying—
from pesticides and cats and loss of forest
habitat and fatal light attraction. In daytime,
songbirds navigate by land. Ancestral
memories of lakes and mountains guide them.
But at night, the only signs they follow
are the stars, and for decades now, electric
lights have turned our cities into artificial
constellations that bewilder them.
They lose sight of the horizon, fly off
course, get lost, and freeze to death.

But most of all they die from slamming
headfirst into high-rise windows. Birds,
the scientists say, don't know what glass is.
They don't understand reflections. Sometimes
late at night we dare to list the things we've lost—
the flocks of bobolinks we don't see anymore,
dancing at the legion, taking the train

through every season of the Qu'Appelle Valley.
And we remember the dark. Our first night
together at the lake, walking downhill
to the beach, our fingers linked, our bare feet
feeling the way, the world invisible until
we made it through the trees. Then the sky
and the lake before us, full of stars.

Now Jupiter has disappeared. The moon
is high and silver. Almost all the stars
are drowned out by that downtown
glare. The birds, we guess, are sleeping.
We douse the fire, enter the house, turn on
the lamps, turn on the stereo. Charlie Hayden's
voice outlives him, just another daily miracle
that shapes our lives, powered by the sun.
Turn off the lights, the scientists advise.
Turn off the lights on the north side
of the buildings so the birds can make it
home. How many will return next year,
in their thin and staggered v-formations,
and who'll be here to greet them?

All night, instead of sleeping, I listen
to your breathing close beside me. Tomorrow,
when you lie on the hospital table,
your chest marked with a felt-pen cross,
your head locked in by the radiation mask,
a technician will guide the fatal beam
into your skull. From ninety-three million
miles away, it will enter your brain,
and maybe you'll hear the birds begin
to sing. Yes, light shines in the darkness,
and still the darkness doesn't have a clue
what's going on. O, world without form,
I remember you, and to you
I am returning.

4

THE READER

Disappointment

how many winter birds have arrived at the empty feeder
since you injured your arm, and what do you say

when your father asks, again, who are these strangers
watering your mother's lily-of-the-valley? uprooting

our centennial tree? is it only politeness that stops you
from reminding him that he is dead, that this moment

is a dream, and by the way it is certainly not summer?

an immigrant, he could never accept that life below zero

is ordinary, that any phenomenon, repeated fifty times,
becomes your life. do you think you are special? do you think

it is only your own husband, who, looking
over your shoulder as you write a poem, mistakes

its shape on the page for a grocery list and believes
you're planning to surprise him

with a birthday dinner?

Poetry Wars

Uptown vs downtown. Borrowers vs thieves.
Metaphysical poets vs poets who don't believe.

20th-century poets vs those from the 21st.
Poets who are drinking vs those with the terrible thirst.

Poets funded by oil vs poets funded by wheat.
Fish vs lumber. Limestone vs peat.

Slam vs dub vs found vs tone.
Bird vs moon. Skin vs bone.

Left-handed poets vs the right.
Day vs day. Night vs night.

Poets who type vs those who erase.
Capitals vs the lower case.

X vs Y. Brain vs heart.
Academia vs art.

Deep as the ocean, old as the stars,
mysterious, furious poetry wars.

Canto of Slinders*

nobody knew who slew
the parachute unfolden
the char perilous, the night
house nude of vellum

canto of slinders: soiled fish
of the sea, the long atlantic slalom

high as kits over the cap, we lip
the opposite of what we lean

the words you crossed out
now who you are
open your own two yes
to the dark dark

* Slinder (n): an error in language, such as a mispronunciation, typo,
or false definition.

First Things

My first husband, melting
margarine in a cast-iron pan,
removes an egg from its cardboard
nest in the refrigerator. Meanwhile,
absorbed in a poem by César Vallejo,
I make a mistake involving a twenty-dollar bill
and a white cat named Pierre. I'm late for work
at the furniture store. I'm nineteen. That's all
you need to know about me. My husband
cradles the egg, cool and almost
weightless in his palm. At the sound
of the doorbell, a shaft of light falls
through the long years, illuminates
his golden curls. The question is,
what's the difference
between an egg and a memory
of an egg? The two men at the door
claim the payments on our stereo are late,
and my first husband lets them in. He lets them.
In. To our apartment. I turn off the gas flame,
follow them all into the living room.
If this were a Hollywood film, I'd pose
them here in a tableau: two bullies
and their innocent victim, still holding
the egg, delicate as an unbroken promise.
He holds it with two hands, one cupped
inside the other.

Only those in the know,
those who have been here
all morning, know the egg is raw,
the book of poems borrowed
from the Sargent Avenue library.
If this were a parable,
I'd speak of the egg as a secret.
I'd say my husband kept a secret
from me, worse than the fact
the stereo wasn't paid for.
If this were a horror movie,

I could tell you
what that secret was.

My husband barely knew me
(no one knew me back then),
but he was aware I hated debt.
He knew I despised finance
companies and their interest
and collection men, those who arrive
at seven in the morning when the stereo
is playing "Dreamboat Annie." Even the stock market,
which most people, back then, thought respectable,
did not escape my contempt. The stereo sang "ship of dreams,"
unaware, in its thing-like mind, that its ownership
was in dispute. It was up to me (so much
was up to me back then) to throw those scoundrels
out of our home before my husband gave up the stereo.
So if this were a story, I'd be the hero,
because I did throw them out.

Meanwhile, the twenty-dollar bill
lay crumpled inside the grocery list
that lay crumpled inside the squashed-flat
cat food tin that was crammed into the bottom
of the garbage can. Yes, that's how hard
I looked for it. Back then, we couldn't afford
to lose twenty dollars. Back then I never gave up.
Never giving up: a family trait
a person can be proud of. In memory,
the egg, caged in my husband's
fingers, seems to glow: the single
blithe, unburdened moment of the day.

Before it cracked open, I'd been tidying
the kitchen, scooping books and papers
from the table-top. My husband
had given me twenty dollars for groceries:
a gift of great significance and love.
But I was absent-minded, careless,

singing "Dreamboat Annie" and feeding Pierre.
I'd crinkled that twenty like a bad first draft (back then,
money was made of paper) and accidentally trashed it.
I looked for it so long I was late for work at the store
where I managed accounts receivable, counting,
always counting, what was owed.

That was the day before the day he told me how it was.
How the men looped the rope around his eight-year-old neck
and fastened it to his ankles before they began to do the things
they did to his body. Because this is a poem,
I can't tell you the rest. I can only repeat the tired lament,
the failure of language, etc. If you ever wish
you'd never been born, look to the egg
(queen of secret-keeping, pope of unbeing). You'll never
read of these things in a literary magazine, and maybe
that's the way it should be, reader dear, for who wants
to witness the fall—the terror that stripped him
to the bone and robbed him of his power,
the way those repo men robbed us
of the elemental things we believed in
when we were first married, sharing
the first meal of the day, a white
cat and a song, first thing
in the morning.

If this were history, it would teach
us something. If it were a riddle,
the answer would be, *no
difference. Unless
you're hungry.*

Concerning Mr. Purdy

1

I read him on the bus, going back and forth
to school in Winnipeg in 1974, getting my bum pinched
in a parable of millponds and lichen while the bus drivers
threatened to strike. My art teacher said I should go to university
and study painting, if I was going to persist in it, seeing as
he didn't want to take all of the blame, and my English teacher
said I should go to university and show my poems
to the professors of writing, because maybe *they* could explain
what was wrong with them. So I went to the U of M.
In English class, we heard there was this guy, a poet
you could show your poems to, that was his job,
and my friends said I should slip some under his door
and run away, but I didn't. I kept the poems to myself,
and one or two boys I was after. They were bad poems,
but the boys liked them, or pretended to, which was all
that mattered. One day in the middle of winter
the professor announced this poet was coming to class to read
to us, and he said the name. He'd never mentioned the name
before. It was a typical day in Winnipeg. Sub-zero torture.
At the campus pub, my friends said I should skip out and stay warm,
but I said no. I went to the classroom early, sat at the front
and rehearsed my request. I wanted to ask him to read "Hombre,"
wanted to hear those words, in the man's own voice, the "five
bloody fingers of Che Guevara." But no one was there
except the students, who talked among themselves
about reading week, which they called skiing week,
and I was justly annoyed until finally, after 15, 20 minutes,
the two of them arrived, the professor and the poet, both of them
tall and handsome and distinguished and dishevelled—
and sitting in the front row, as I was, I could smell
the beer. They stood behind the podium and spoke
to each other, continuing a conversation
they'd been nursing all afternoon in the campus pub,
where I should have stayed, I guess, and then
the professor looked at us as if he'd just remembered
we were there, though he wasn't sure why,

and he introduced the poet, one of Canada's
most important writers, he said, though of course, he said,
none of *us* had ever heard of him. I remember his tone acutely,
"none of *you* could care less." And he laughed.
They both laughed, scornful, brave, and unappreciated,
surrounded by spoiled brats, the children of Philistines,
wasting their time on this little fart of a gig, this day job,
never guessing someone might be sitting there, someone
might have been sitting there a long time, waiting for a poem,
and I was sad, for I was a sensitive girl.

2

I went west, though not on a boxcar. I stood on the highway
with my thumb outstretched, and at night I looked at the stars
and thought, the road at night is beauty if you got that kinda mind
which I ain't. I had given up on writing. I got a job digging clams
and hung around with the other fishermen, and sometimes
I read poems to them—not my own poems, for I had given up
on men for the most part, too, and anyway these guys smelled
like fish—but I read them poems out of the books I had,
and their favourite poem was "At the Quinte Hotel."
Then one day at the Campbell River library we saw a poster
saying he was coming to town, and I said I had met him,
well sort of, in Winnipeg, and Don, the herring boat captain,
said we should all go hear him read and afterwards take him
to the Quinsam Hotel in town, which is just like the Quinte Hotel
in his poem and even starts with a Q, and Norman said, hey,
it probably *was* the Quinsam Hotel where that happened,
sounds just like it, and writers are always changing the names
of places. They convinced themselves that this was true.
The night of the reading, we all squeezed into the back
of Dennis's pickup and drove to this little community hall
where about twelve people we'd never seen before were sitting
on folding chairs, and when we entered in our rubber boots
and mud and checkered flannel, smoking our roll-your-owns—
you could smoke anywhere back then, or we thought you could—
this lady came up and told us, sorry, we were in the wrong place,

what place were we looking for, and we said here, and she said,
you know there is going to be poetry? Read out loud? For an hour?
It was a good reading and when it was over we all clapped and then
the lady asked if there were any questions, and I put up my hand.
He hadn't read "Hombre," and I thought maybe he would if
I asked him, but the lady took a question from someone else instead
and soon they were all asking questions about landscape
and the nation, and this went on for a while, and I could see
he was tired, so I put down my hand. Afterwards,
Don went up to the front and waited outside the little circle
of people. Don was as tall as the poet, and even though
all these people were between them, the people were short.
I heard Don ask him if he wanted to come for a beer,
but the lady asked please could we wait outside a few minutes,
as she had to lock up, and she locked up all right.
The minute we stepped outside, she locked the door,
and soon we heard a car start in the lot out back,
and saw them drive right past us.
He was in the front seat beside her, the collar
of his trench coat pulled up high. "Jeez," said Dennis,
"what a stuck-up maddened bitch, the poor guy,"
and Don said, "got a smoke?" and I stood there growing older.

3

Don's dead now, knifed through the gut, and Norman drowned
on the herring run, and the poet lived a good long life and died,
though his words remain, and me
I'm back in school, and once in a while
I show a poem to someone,
but it's not the same. This afternoon I listened to the CD
he recorded in 1998, and "Hombre" is not on it,
and it's too late now, to ask for anything.
His voice quavers, and sometimes, listening, I get angry
at him, who does he think he is, getting old like that
and telling us stuff we already know, like a poem won't really
buy beer or flowers, duh, or a goddam thing, though by now
I can't remember where I picked that up in the first place—

maybe it was from him after all, that little paperback
with the forest on the cover, c.1972, the one I read
on the bus, yes. And I realize, despite the quaver, that the cadence
is still strong, after 600 years, the ivory thought is still warm,
and suddenly I'd like to hear every damn poem. He had a way
of telling a poem, as if it was about something else, flowers
maybe, or the Dorsets, or Milton Acorn, but always the poem
was the story of his own life, and maybe
I picked that up too. And maybe P.S. he was wrong,
because maybe a poem can buy flowers, or at least
give them to us: the yellow flowers in the beer,
the noisy flowers of the Arctic, that white blossom
of frost at Portage and Main, the five bloody fingers
of Che Guevera, blooming in the hand,
and the first flowers ever, a hundred million years ago,
the thousand thousand flowers covering our tracks.

Reading Treasure Island

I was twenty years old when I found *Treasure Island*
in a free store on Gabriola and took it with me
to Cortes, where I planned to read it at night
by the light of an oil lamp in a canvas tent.
That was the year I deserted my first husband
when he needed me most. I had no money.
I hitchhiked west until I hit the ocean
and then I looked for work up island,
where I had some friends.

I didn't know my husband had borrowed a car
and come out to the coast to find me. He followed
me north up the Island Highway, and news of his coming
preceded him. Friends said he'd been seen in Qualicum
Beach, then Parksville, then Campbell River, where,
they said, he swallowed so much whisky
he fell into a bonfire. The burn left a scar
I didn't see for seven years.

While Jim Hawkins kept his weather-eye open
for a seafaring man with one leg, I pitched my tent high
on a rocky ridge above the long inlet that nearly slices
Cortes in two. I had friends with me,
and a wooden boat named *Walrus*, over-powered
by a 40-horse Johnson. At low tide, I'd beach her
on the rocky shore, tied to an arbutus. At high tide,
I anchored her out deep and swam to shore.
I was the only one who could swim that far.
We were all hiding out, from a husband or a debt
or a warrant for failure to appear, and we figured
we'd make a living digging clams.

While my husband recovered from his burns
in a Campbell River motel, Jim Hawkins
was meeting Mr. Silver at the sign of the Spy-glass.
Tall American yachts sailed into the inlet.
On the fourth of July they lit the sky with gold
and silver trails of fire and the sounds
of war. I wasn't worried about Jim. All I knew
of Stevenson was *A Child's Garden of Verse*.

We dug clams all day, collecting them in big net bags
and storing them in the shade below the tide line
until we could get them to the docks to sell.
I went back and forth in *Walrus*, selling clams
and gathering supplies. The rest of the time
I slept or swam or read. There was a mossy outcrop
shaped like an easy chair, high on the edge
of the cliff, a perfect precipice for readers.
Or when the tide was low, I'd walk to the reading rock,
a long flat mottled bed of granite in the middle of the inlet,
where I could lie in the sun. My husband,
who was already lost—I had already lost him—came
closer and closer, and though we never spoke, both of us
believed the reunion would bring forth some consequence.
Neither of us knew where I was going, or why.

One evening I returned late from the docks.
It was dark when I entered the inlet
near our campsite. I cut the motor and drifted
in silence. At the top of the cliff, the tent glowed
yellow. I saw the shadows of my friends move
across the canvas, heard their words.
I wanted to be with them and I wanted to be alone
in the boat, listening to their voices lilt and laugh
and lift across the water. The dark ocean brimmed.
I knew it was open to receive me.

The next day, my friends looked down
from the cliff top and saw my husband
hiking toward us through the woods
across the bay. I took *Treasure Island*
and waded out to the reading rock.
The water was up to my knees and coming in fast.
By the time my husband arrived, Jim Hawkins
and me were surrounded on all sides
by deep salt water. Nobody could touch us.
I lay on my belly and read all day. I'd seen
the tide charts and knew I had plenty of time.

When Jim and the crew reached Treasure Island,
things got ugly. I wasn't expecting these gruesome scenes
of death and mutilation in a kids' book. But I was committed
now. Eventually the voices of my friends carried
across the water as they greeted my husband.
I didn't turn around. Long John Silver's men had handed him
the black spot. Things were heating up, and now that I knew
they could get worse, I paid attention. Silver turned
the black spot over and read the word on the other side:
"Deposed." I lay one side of my face down on the open pages,
closed my eyes. I was on a rock in the middle of the inlet
and I didn't know what "deposed" meant. I felt the sun rise
higher, heat soaking into my spine. I lay there for a long time,
trying not to think, and then suddenly two young guys
in a rowboat came by, only ten feet from my rock, rowing so quietly
I didn't know they were there, until they were there.
We talked for about half a minute, as they glided by
and I showed them the way to the waterfall.
Then as they moved away, I asked,
"What does *deposed* mean?"
And the younger one told me. The tide
was as high as it was going to get that day.
It would be hours before anyone
could reach me. To be deposed
meant to lose your place. Now that I knew,
I kept on reading.

Reading Strangers

At dawn I revisit the Anita Brookner novel
I was reading yesterday, ignoring the scraps
of scribbled poems our guests left scattered
on the dinner table after last night's recitations,
and the cold pan of grease on the stove, still
fragrant with olives and thyme. Fiona the cat
complains, *the house is empty*. She's sociable,
Fiona is, black as the last three cats, but blacker
and more lonely, prone to merowling into the void
of one or two or four a.m. As the sky begins
to pale, she surrenders at last, settling like a coil
into a cushion on the couch. I'm opening the curtains.
Anyone who's ever spent a winter on the long plains
this far north will understand. We're two weeks
past the winter solstice, and the light's returning,
imperceptibly. It's time to read. Years ago,
Brookner and Drabble and Lessing surprised me
with a concept I encountered late in life,
that a woman's shaped by her social position
among social persons, that clothes and manners
count, that a person might care
what stupid people think, might feel shame
if not attractive. My mother never
wasted a minute on these ideas, would not
even have graced them with the name *ideas*.
Looks are not important, she told me, and believed it.
She was kind to everyone and secretly snubbed snobs.
And yet I like to read the party scenes in Drabble's novels,
enjoy the little power struggles of those not quite elite.
I like parties, especially in our own house. Friends
who get dressed up and brave the snow to come here
with their poems, guitars, and arguments.
There's warmth in Drabble, if not depth enough to please me.
But Brookner strips life bare: damp English winters,
duty, chilly chores and cold sores, the stupor
of a woman's servitude. And yet of all the women
I've met in Brookner's novels, there are none
so lonely as Paul Sturgis, with his fish-like name

and indecision. May I say he breaks my heart
with the simple quest he's on, the one he doesn't
understand. What is it to be lonely? Maybe I've missed it,
with my life-long love of reading, my lack of appreciation
for the surface of things. I close the book a moment,
just to think, and the amaryllis my stepson gave us
whispers suddenly into the silent house, its bud
unfurling with a sound like the turning of a page.

The Following

the oxygen immerses me
the blue light
the clear atoms
of our human air
—from "Diving into the Wreck" by Adrienne Rich

When I finally follow you down,
it's late. The stars are dark
over lit-up Baltimore. Yes, I know
what the ladder's for. All my life
I've been descending these ragged
rungs toward the surface of the sea,
and now I'm ready for the dive.
I slide between your lines, slip
through the night air easily;
the oxygen immerses me,

then lets me go. Down, down
through the bioluminescent bloom,
you beckoned those of us who read
the book of myths. You led us through
the underwater underworld to look
at the crime scene, the gravesite,
the wreck. You said we could breathe again
after the hanging, the drowning, the rape.
You said we could write.
The blue light

of cities can't penetrate here.
Whatever we gather, we gather
in the dark. The beauty in the ruins
is the ruins. Whatever our losses, we are
what remains: stripped vessel
and gliding shark, the bones of the ones
who came before. The eye pearls, shut
as seashells, of the mermaid who sings
no more. The cold that numbs,
the clear atoms

of water, the salt that stings. Enough.
I grasp the lines you cast, begin
to climb. I'm not alone. I see the others,
in the bay and all along the eastern shore.
On every coast, in every inland lake,
they're rising through the layers,
up to the sunlit strata, where
they surface, gasping
to inhale their share
of our human air.

The Haunting

But when you feel longing, sing of women in love;
for their famous passion is still not immortal. Sing
of women abandoned and desolate (you envy them, almost)
who could love so much more purely than those who were gratified.
—from *Duino Elegies* by Rainer Maria Rilke,
translated by Stephen Mitchell

Who, if I cried out, might pluck me from this dark
suburban solitude? George Bowering is no comfort
at such moments. As for those who haunt the bookcase—Rilke,
Milosz, Shelley, Yeats, Neruda, Mandelstam—all night
they're wide awake, though dead, rehearsing
ars poeticas and importuning muses in the air above
my bed. Gentlemen, go right ahead. When you write
of valour, speak of blood; when you engage in argument,
deploy that cold articulation you're so certain of.
But when you feel longing, sing of women in love;

for nothing moves you so like female pain, nothing pulls
the music from your throats like women's mourning.
Otherwise, there's just the void—inscrutable scrim of stars,
that one tree on the hill. And Rilke, as you've said, our minds
can't apprehend the world of animals, or angels, or the dead
(though you're longing to be crushed by mighty wings),
worlds where meanings come apart like untied strings. Poets,
begin with simple praise. Quote the sky, the voices of the wind.
But if you aspire to greatness, sing of women suffering,
for their famous passion is still not immortal. Sing

to glorify us for posterity, as only you guys can. Dear Rilke,
can we say who turned to whom, tonight? When gripped
by wild insomnia, I opened up your books and hoped
to unlock sleep. Instead, I found there words that deepened
my own grief. And when I rose to sort the midnight laundry,
wash my absent husband's socks, you followed, taking notes
on wifely chores, the pitch and pulse of female loneliness.
Was this how you practised to describe those numinous figurines
who glide across the landscape of Lament? The beautiful ghosts
of women abandoned and desolate (you envy them, almost).

You envy them their full completion, which you envision as a love
that soars above all things. But brother, I forgive your male imaginings.
Let us each compose our elegies, you on the windy bastions of Duino
Castle, me in the coffee shop of St. Boniface General Hospital. Let
my ordinary language live between your lines. For what I'm losing,
I am losing here, on Earth, not in those other worlds, that other side
where you have so poetically dissolved. Leave me my imperfect troubles,
my empty bungalow, my dusty books. Go after what you really want:
the women with clean pain, the mothers of heroes, the widowed brides,
who could love so much more purely than those who were gratified.

The Reader

> *But now it is she who pauses,*
> *As if to reject my thought and its easy figure.*
> *A stillness greatens, in which*
> *The whole house seems to be thinking.*
> —from "The Writer" by Richard Wilbur

I'm the girl behind the door in Richard Wilbur's poem,
typing in solitude. Confinement frees me
from my family. The sentences I make are blades,
the brash clatter of the keys a song: I'm getting out!
Wilbur invented this scene of writing: the daughter,
the typing, the shut door, the linden that tosses
against the window, the bird as metaphor, his own paused
self interpreting her keystrokes as a kind of battle.
What does he know of her writing and its causes?
But now it is she who pauses

to question my intrusion in her home. How can I compare
myself to her? I'm the parent, listening on the stair
to the rhythms that my daughter makes. I long
to hold her captive in the house of words I've built
to keep her safe. Instead, I open the casement,
brace myself for the coming, necessary rupture.
It arrives with all the breathless grace and power
of a prisoner released. I watch her as she turns
away from me and strides into her future,
as if to reject my thought and its easy figure.

I'm the bird in the room, the frightened starling
fluttering hard against the window glass. *Wild,*
he called me, *sleek* and *iridescent.* Yes, I fled too early
from my parents' house and recognized too late
that grief would lodge like fire in my throat,
that I'd be haunted and bewitched
and typing hard through every night. And now,
in a house of books, with neither parents nor child,
where the doors lock, and the clock ticks,
a stillness greatens, in which

I'm only the reader of the poem. It cuts me twice,
with its escaping and its letting go. This morning,
news of Wilbur's death lands hard on the frozen doorstep
in the dark, and I take down his book, reread the poem
I've lived inside for forty years, as I live in this house,
alone and typing, sometimes drinking,
while the stillness swells in the cold air, fills
the empty rooms until there's no sound anywhere.
Only winter closing in, and the mercury sinking.
The whole house seems to be thinking.

ACKNOWLEDGEMENTS

Some of these pieces have appeared, often in earlier versions, in the following journals and anthologies: *Cyclops Review*, CV2, *Prairie Fire*, *Matrix, Best Canadian Poems 2013, Best Canadian Poems 2014, A/Cross Sections: New Manitoba Writing, Post-Prairie: An Anthology of New Writing, Scratching the Surface: The Post-Prairie Landscape, The Echoing Years: An Anthology of Poetry from Canada and Ireland.* Thanks to CV2 and *Prairie Fire*, several of these poems have been nominated for awards.

Many editors and curators of other kinds have published or hosted parts of this work at readings or in other ways, and some wonderful artists have inspired and supported me during the writing of these poems. Thanks to Clive Holden, Ron Robinson, Kevin Higgins, Susan Millar DuMars, Katherine Bitney, Andris Taskans, Charlene Diehl, Clarise Foster, Colin Smith, Steven Matijcio, Kelly Hughes, Jon Paul Fiorentino, the late Robert Kroetsch, Mary Reid, Mary di Michele, Sue Goyette, Molly Peacock, Jake Mooney, Stephanie McKenzie, Randall Maggs, John Ennis, Karen Haughian, Méira Cook, Scott Nolan, Glenn Buhr, Margaret Sweatman, Barbara Schott, and Melody Morrissette. Special thanks to my editor for *St. Boniface Elegies*, Garry Thomas Morse. Thanks also to Cliff Eyland for allowing us to feature his gorgeous painting *Low Level NATO Flight over Labrador* on the cover. And thanks to the National University of Ireland in Galway, the Banff Centre, and the University of Winnipeg. I'm blessed.

"Chatham Beach" and "Holiday"
These poems are for Anne Marie Resta.

"Oodena"
This poem remembers Doreen Hunter, George Morrissette, and Patrick O'Connell.

"Winter Archive"
This piece was inspired by Wanda Koop's brilliant series of paintings, *Satellite City*.

"The News"
This whole section remembers Ron Schneider.

"Collaborations"
For his *Fly by Night* project in 2016, New York artist Duke Riley attached LED lights to the ankles of two thousand homing pigeons he had trained with flags and whistles. He then appears to conduct their flight at sunset over the Brooklyn Navy Yards. According to a *New York Times* article by Andy Newman, "The pigeons are trained only to return eventually to the ship, not to fly specific patterns; their choreography is entirely their own" ("2,000 Pigeons Will Put on a Light Show in Brooklyn" posted April 28, 2016 at www.nytimes.com/2016/04/29/arts/design/-duke-riley-pigeons-fly-by-night.html).

Other information and the quotations in this poem come from Emily Rhyne's article "In Brooklyn, Pigeons Light Up the Sky" and her video *Flight of the Pigeon*, both posted by *The New Yorker* on June 13, 2016, at www.newyorker.com/culture/culture-desk/in-brooklyn-pigeons-light-up-the-sky.

And if you haven't yet heard Carl Sandburg reading his story "How Six Pigeons Came Back to Hatrack the Horse After Many Accidents and Six Telegrams," I highly recommend listening to it. Maybe it's on YouTube.

"Canto of Slinders"

The phrase "soiled fish of the sea," from the novel *White-Jacket*, by Herman Melville, was a typographical error made famous by the critic F. O. Matthiessen. The other typos in this poem have less distinguished origins, usually my own emails.

"Concerning Mr. Purdy"

Poems by Al Purdy that are quoted, riffed on, or ripped off in this piece include: "Concerning Ms Atwood," "Dylan," "Say the Names," "A Typical Day in Winnipeg," "Arctic Rhododendrons," "Trees at the Arctic Circle," "Transient," "Home," "In the Early Cretaceous," "Home-Made Beer," "House Guest," "Seasons," "The Sculptors," "Lament for the Dorsets," "The Following," "At the Quinte Hotel," and of course "Hombre."

Catherine Hunter's earlier poetry collection *Latent Heat* won the McNally Robinson Manitoba Book of the Year Award, and four of the poems in *St. Boniface Elegies*, published earlier in CV2, won the Manitoba Magazine Award for Best Poem or Suite of Poems and earned Honourable Mention in the National Magazine Awards. Her recent novel *After Light* (Signature) spans four generations of an Irish-American-Canadian family in a tale of love, war, trauma, and the power of art. She has also published several mysteries with Ravenstone/Turnstone, and recorded a spoken word CD (*Rush Hour*, from Cyclops Press, with a bonus track by The Weakerthans). Her writing has also appeared in numerous journals and anthologies. She edited *Exposed*, an anthology of five new women poets, and *Before the First Word: The Poetry of Lorna Crozier*, and for ten years she was the editor of The Muses' Company poetry press. Since 1991, she has enjoyed teaching literature and creative writing at the University of Winnipeg.